The Library of
E-Commerce and Internet Careers

Careers
as a
Content Provider
for
the Web

Erin M. Hovanec

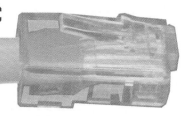

The Rosen Publishing Group, Inc.
New York

Published in 2001 by The Rosen Publishing Group, Inc.
29 East 21st Street, New York, NY 10010

First Edition

Library of Congress Cataloging-in-Publication Data

Hovanec, Erin M.
Careers as a content provider for the web / Erin M. Hovanec.
— 1st ed.
p. cm. — (The library of e-commerce and internet careers)
Includes bibliographical references and index.
ISBN 0-8239-3418-7 (lib. bdg.)
1. Electronic commerce—Vocational guidance—Juvenile literature. 2. Internet industry—Vocational guidance—Juvenile literature. [1. Electronic commerce—Vocational guidance. 2. Web site development industry—Vocational guidance. 3. Vocational guidance.] I. Title. II. Series.
HF5548.32 .H68 2001
658.8'4—dc21

2001000088

Manufactured in the United States of America

Table of Contents

Introduction — 4

1 Why Do We Need E-Commerce Content? — 6

2 Types of E-Commerce Content — 17

3 Careers Creating Content — 27

4 Careers Working with Content — 36

5 Is an E-Commerce Content Career for You? — 46

Glossary — 54

For More Information — 57

For Further Reading — 60

Index — 62

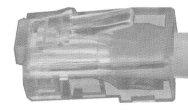

Introduction

I t may be difficult to believe, but only a decade ago, very few people worked with the Internet. A handful of scientists and computer experts were busy shaping the technology that would forever change the lives of people around the world. Times have changed. Today, Internet companies employ millions of people. By 2002, the number of Web pages is expected to reach eight billion—a number greater than the world's population.

The most explosive area of Internet growth has been in e-commerce. Web sites that sell products such as books or automobiles or services such as travel reservations are called e-commerce sites. An increasing number of people are making purchases over the Internet, and e-commerce is becoming an enormous—and very profitable—industry. Of all U.S. adults who use the Internet, 56 percent shop online. Adults aren't the only online shoppers, however. By 2005, teenagers are expected to spend $4.9 billion online each year.

In order to attract customers to their site, convince them to make a purchase, and encourage repeat business, e-commerce companies need interesting, informative, and sometimes provocative content. Content is much more than just the written word. It's the many elements that combine to make a site, including text, images, audio, video, and community. E-commerce sites feature all types of content, from product descriptions and images of merchandise to sound and video clips.

"E-Business: A disruptive change in the course of commerce that will reward those who embrace it and punish those who try to avoid it."
—*Business Week* **Magazine**

As the number of e-commerce Web sites increases, so does the demand for content. E-businesses are trying to keep up with the demand by creating fresh and useful content to market their products and services. E-commerce content providers are always looking for creative, intelligent people to join them.

Why Do We Need E-Commerce Content?

IN THE BEGINNING . . .

When people talk about the Internet, they're usually referring to the World Wide Web. When they talk about Internet content, they usually mean text, or the written word. That's because, for a long time, text was the only kind of content available on the Web. As the Web developed, people began to realize that the Web had vast potential. They saw that it could do much more than simply provide information; it could also sell products and services. And e-commerce was born.

Simply, e-commerce is the practice of selling goods and services over the Internet. E-commerce Web sites can be as large as Amazon.com, the first notable online retailer, or e-tailer, which offers millions of products and services to over 20 million customers worldwide, or as small as a personal site that an amateur artist has built himself or herself. E-commerce has come a long way since its beginnings in the early to mid-1990s. Today, hundreds of thousands of e-commerce sites sell every sort of product. And Amazon.com is the Web's leading shopping site, offering everything from cars to books to electronics and serving customers in 160 countries.

E-commerce sales can be categorized into two types: business-to-consumer and business-to-business. Business-to-consumer (B2C) sales are those in which a company sells a product or service to an individual for his or her own use. For example, if you go to Gap.com and purchase a pair of jeans, the site makes a business-to-consumer sale. The U.S. Commerce Department predicts that U.S. consumer e-commerce is expected to reach $269 billion by 2005.

Business-to-business (B2B) sales are those in which a company sells a product or service to another company. For example, if your school logs on to Ringor's Web site and purchases new uniforms for the softball team, that site makes a business-to-business sale. According to Jupiter Research, the premier Internet research firm, U.S. business-to-business e-commerce will rise to $6.3 trillion in 2005, from $336

Many e-tailers, such as buy.com, sell to both consumers (called B2C e-commerce) and other companies (called B2B e-commerce).

billion in 2000. Although many companies specialize in one type of sale, others, like buy.com, sell to both consumers and businesses.

As you can see from these predictions, e-commerce is expected to grow explosively in the next few years in both business sectors. More brick-and-mortar companies (retailers that have a physical storefront as well as a Web site) such as K-mart and Wal-Mart have created very successful e-commerce sites. These companies and many others like them will all need skilled employees. That's where you come in.

WHY E-COMMERCE COMPANIES WANT—AND NEED!—CONTENT

Most people agree that content is the most important part of an e-commerce Web site. It's the key to making the site a success. Of course, sites should look attractive and be easy to navigate. But most important, they should have clear, useful, and correct information—no matter what form that information takes. When people go to a site, they're usually looking for specific content. Getting them to the site and keeping them there is an important part of a successful e-commerce strategy. Strong content that encourages repeat sales, coupled with clear and easy navigation, is a surefire recipe for success.

> "We know an awful lot about the customers. We know their addresses, their shopping habits, their preferences."
> **—Terrell Jones, CEO Travelocity.com, on how to keep customers loyal**

E-commerce Web sites' number one goal is to make a sale. They make their money by selling products or services to their customers. If you've ever made a purchase online, you know that it's very different from buying something in a store. You can't pick up the object, turn it around, and touch it. You

Teens and the Web

When it comes to Internet smarts, today's teenagers are the smartest generation ever.

► 70 percent of students with online access say they use the Internet at least once a week from home or school.

► 35 percent of students with online access report using the Internet almost every day.

► Students with online access spend almost seven hours per month online.

► 63 percent of U.S. public school classrooms had Internet access by the end of 1999.

can't ask a salesperson to answer your questions. Instead, you have to rely on the information on your computer screen. For these reasons, online content is very important. Product descriptions have to be clear. Images have to be accurate and attractive. Audio and video must show off the product to its best advantage. The elements of the online content have to work well together to turn a browser (someone just window-shopping online) into a buyer.

E-commerce companies also want people to return to their Web sites again and again. The more times a person visits, the more likely it is that he or she will make a purchase. Content helps to keep people coming back by enhancing a site's "stickiness." The stickier a Web site is, the longer a visitor remains there, and the more likely he or she is to "bookmark" that site and return. Each individual person who visits a site is recorded as a unique visitor. Companies with many unique visitors can attract advertisers who'll pay to post ads on their site. As a visitor keeps clicking around the site, the company records which pages the person is visiting. If that person clicks on a product to find out more, the site records that as a "click through." Advertisers look carefully at click-through rates when deciding on which site to spend their money.

Many e-commerce companies are also using contextual commerce to sell their products. Contextual commerce puts commerce into context by selling products that relate to the content. For example, a movie review might allow viewers to purchase other movies featuring the same actors or the book on which the film was based. Using content and contextual commerce, content creators and providers are helping to shape the future of e-commerce.

Content is a very powerful force in a Web site, and it can make an e-commerce site a success or a failure. The best content will hold a person's interest

Content creators often meet and brainstorm ideas for the development of exciting interactive Web pages.

and offer information, as well as encourage him or her to return.

WHAT IS CONTENT ANYWAY?

By now you may be wondering, "If content isn't just text, than what exactly *is* it?" Well, content is all the individual pieces that combine to make a Web site. The most common type of content is text. Images such as illustrations, photographs, and computer-designed creations are also content, as are audio and video. Finally, community is perhaps the most under-appreciated type of content. Community refers to features such as chat rooms and bulletin boards. It allows a site's visitors to communicate with one another and create their own content.

One thing that content is *not* are applets. Applets are very small computer programs, such as games and calculators, that reside on a Web page. Applets do help to make up a Web page, and they do provide information. However, rather than being a piece of visual or audio information, they're actually pro-grams. As programs, they're created in a very differ-ent way than traditional content.

CREATING CONTENT VERSUS PROVIDING CONTENT

If you're interested in a career as a content provider, the first thing you'll need to understand is that creating content and providing content are two different things. People who create content do things such as write or edit text, take photographs, draw illustrations, record audio, shoot video or film, and design Web pages. Without them, Internet content would not exist.

Other people provide content that has been created by someone else. They may change that content to fit the needs of the Web site, but they're working with someone else's creation. Jobs in this field include content strategists and producers. It's their job to discover exactly what sort of content a site needs and then search for it. Web developers, who combine all sorts of content to create pages and sites, are also content providers. Rich media (animation, video, or audio) producers decide how to best use pieces of digital audio or video on a site. Finally, community managers provide content by organizing bulletin boards on sites and running chats to encourage visitors to talk with one another and create "user-generated" content.

Lastly, some people work for companies that provide content that has been created by others. These companies are sometimes called content syndicators. They get content from one place, like a newspaper or a photographer, and give it to a site that needs that particular type of content. Two companies that do this very successfully are ScreamingMedia and iSyndicate. These companies don't actually create content themselves, but they do a very important job of supplying content.

saksfifthavenue.com

Back | Forward | Stop | Refresh | Home | AutoFill | Print | Mail

Address: http://www.saksfifthavenue.com/Entry.jsp?FOLDER%3C%3Efolder_id=42537&ASSORTMENT%3C%3East_id=41385&bmUID=982174959239&G

Live Home Page | Apple Computer | Apple Support | Apple Store | MSN | Office for Macintosh | Internet Explorer

WOMEN MEN CHILDREN **GIFTS**   LIVE HELP   SEARCH

SAKS FIFTH AVENUE

DESIGNER BOUTIQUE / FUR SALON
APPAREL
PETITES
SALON Z: SIZES 14 TO 24
SHOES
HANDBAGS / ACCESSORIES
JEWELRY
INTIMATE APPAREL / HOSIERY
COSMETICS / FRAGRANCES
SALE

SAKS FIFTH AVENUE GIFTS

SHOP BY TREND

SALE

FOR BABY

FOR HOSTESS & GUEST

SAKS COLLECTION

VALENTINE'S DAY

FOR WOMEN

WEDDINGS & ANNIVERSARY

FOR THE HOME

CORPORATE

FOR MEN

Critics wonder if consumers will spend hundreds of dollars to buy things over the Internet that they cannot first inspect.

E-COMMERCE CASE STUDY: SAKS FIFTH AVENUE

In August 2000, retailer Saks Fifth Avenue launched an e-commerce Web site: saksfifthavenue.com. Stores like Neiman Marcus, Bloomingdale's, and Lord & Taylor had had mixed success with e-tailing, and Saks was determined to be more successful. Saks faced a singular challenge: create content that was compelling and powerful enough to persuade viewers to purchase costly items based only on the information on its site. The Saks Fifth Avenue site sells over 12,000 items from leading designers, some costing more than $1,000. Saks claims that the site will allow people to shop whenever and from wherever they want, and will reach markets not served by Saks's brick-and-mortar stores. But critics claim that a Web site can't pamper customers in the way that Saks's stores do, and customers won't spend hundreds of dollars on an item that they can't handle. Who's correct? It's too early to tell.

Types of
E-Commerce Content

Whether you're a writer or an artist, a musician or a computer whiz, or even simply a great communicator, you'll fit right into the world of e-commerce content.

THE WRITTEN WORD

The most basic—and most familiar—type of content is text. The Internet started as text, and most Web sites still contain more text than any other type of content. There are many kinds of text, each serving a different function.

Marketing text, or "copy," is used to promote a product, service, or idea. It's usually very persuasive and tries to convince you to share the author's point of view. On e-commerce sites, the marketing copy is similar to the copy you see in catalogs. It describes the product or service and hopes to persuade you to buy it. When you log on to a music site to check out the latest CDs, the text that describes them is marketing copy.

Instructional copy is used to teach a skill or to show someone how to complete a task. E-commerce Web sites utilize instructional copy to explain how to navigate the site, place an order, or find an item. Some e-commerce sites also employ instructional copy on their sites to encourage people to visit in the hopes that they'll purchase something. For example, Cooking.com, a cookware and kitchen gadget e-tailer, presents recipes side-by-side with items for sale.

Informational copy presents just that—information. It tells you about a place, person, or event, and often presents an objective point of view. E-commerce Web sites usually feature informational copy in their "About Us" section or corporate profile. There you can find information about the company, its management, its mission statement, and its history.

You'll need to remember another important thing about online text: not all of it was created to be on the Web. In fact, a great deal of online content was first meant for the printed page! E-tailers often "re-purpose" or re-use text from their mail order catalogs on their e-commerce sites. Sometimes this strategy doesn't work very effectively. Content created for the printed page can be very different from content created for the Web.

IMAGES

Images are another very common type of content. Just about every Web page today features images. Picture your favorite e-commerce site without any images. Is it less appealing? Sort of boring? Probably. And would you purchase an item from a site if it didn't offer a photograph of it? Probably not. Images are a crucial component of any Web site.

There are three types of images that you'll see most often on the Web. The first is the digital photographs. Digital photographs are pictures that have been converted to a digital format—a format that allows a computer to display them. Before digital cameras, people often took a photograph with a camera, copied it into their computer using a scanner, and then displayed it on the Web. Today, however, photographers can use a digital camera to take a photograph that is Web-ready. Digital cameras save each photograph as an image file that a content creator can then move to a computer and place on a Web page—all within minutes. E-commerce sites often use digital photographs to show an item "in the real world." Sporting goods e-tailers, for example, use live, exciting action shots of equipment to entice you to purchase it.

At bn.com, there are numerous product shots, which are computer-generated images of items for sale.

On the Web, you'll also find online illustrations. Illustrations can be as simple as a hand-drawn diagram or as complicated as an architect's blueprints. Some illustrations are created on paper and scanned into a computer, but most are created online. Graphic artists use programs like Freehand and Adobe Illustrator to draw onscreen what they once would have had to draw by hand on paper.

The third type of image—and the most common—is the computer-generated image. Computer-generated images can be a combination of an actual image on paper, a traditional or digital photograph, and/or an illustration. What makes these images unique is that they have been either entirely created or significantly altered using a computer. Simple computer-generated images include wallpaper (the image that appears faintly behind the other elements on a Web page), page borders, buttons (where a customer is directed to "point and click"), and logos. "Product shots," images of items for sale, are usually computer-generated images. If you log on to BN.com, you'll see computer-generated images of books, videos, CDs, and other products.

AUDIO

Web site sounds are called analog waves. Computers, however, read digital sound waves. Through a process called digital sampling, you can use a computer to convert an analog sound wave to a digital one. The computer can then "read" the digital sound wave. To play the wave, it first reads the digital file and then converts the wave back to an analog wave, so that your ear is able to hear it. Digital audio files can take several formats, including AU, AIFF, WAVE, and MPEG.

E-commerce Web sites usually use audio files very sparingly because the files are often large, and

E-Commerce Hot Shot

Jason Olim, president, CEO, and cofounder of CDNOW

When Jason Olim started CDNOW in his parents' basement, he had no idea of what was to come. Jason had gotten a bachelor's degree in computer science from Brown University in 1992 and had worked as a software engineer for two years. In August 1994, he and his twin brother, Matt, created CDNOW with the goal of making online music fun and easy to find. Today, CDNOW is a leading entertainment Web site that offers everything from music to entertainment merchandise to exclusive interviews. Early in its development, CDNOW used audio content to entice and entertain viewers and, ultimately, to encourage sales. In September 2000, Bertelsmann AG, the third largest media company in the world, acquired CDNOW. Jason stayed with the company as its president, CEO, and cofounder. His once tiny company had finally made it big!

most sites don't need them to sell a product. If a visitor is using a slow modem connection to the Internet, the data can't travel to the computer very quickly. If it takes a long time for that person to download the sound file to the computer, he or she may give up and click to another site. For that reason, it's very important that sound files be compressed, or shrunk, as small as possible before adding them to a Web site. Sites that sell CDs, videos, DVDs, and other kinds of entertainment merchandise often include sound or video clips. Viewers use the clips to sample the product before buying it.

VIDEO

Digital video is a very exciting part of Web technology. Although it's a field that is changing as fast as the Web, certain basic principles apply. Analog video, just like analog audio, must be converted to a digital format before a computer can read it. To best understand digital video, think of it as a series of images called frames. The computer records each of these frames and plays them back in order. The process works much like those old cartoon flipbooks. The computer shows you many separate images one after another, but at a very fast pace, so that you see one image that changes continuously.

23

Students at East Grand Rapids High School chat with college admissions officials during the Online College Fair at the school in October 2000.

Because digital video files are also very big, most sites currently show only short video clips. These clips range from several minutes to just a few seconds. If you've ever viewed a newspaper online, you've likely seen a digital video accompanying an article.

Most e-commerce sites don't need video to sell their products. However, many entertainment sites may use video clips to promote a CD, video, or DVD.

COMMUNITY

Community is probably the least used type of content on e-commerce Web sites, but it can be one of the most important. An online community is a lot like a physical community: People come together because they have a shared interest or activity. The most popular kinds of online communities are chat rooms and bulletin boards (also called message boards or usenets). E-commerce sites use community to bring visitors to their Web sites. Community encourages people to meet and get involved. That way, those people will keep coming back to the Web site and will hopefully make an eventual purchase.

Chat rooms are places on the Internet where you can talk in real time with a live person. You take turns typing, just as you would take turns talking in a live conversation. People go to chat rooms to make friends, get information about topics, and even talk with celebrities. A chat-room monitor also attends the chat room and listens (or watches) the conversation to ensure that the discussion remains on the topic (if the chat is about a specific issue) and that everyone behaves politely. E-commerce sites hold chats for one major reason: to drive traffic to their Web sites. By hosting a celebrity chat or building a community, they may increase the number of visitors. They hope that at least some of those visitors will eventually make purchases.

Online bulletin boards are much like the bulletin boards you see in your classrooms at school. They're places within a Web site where people post messages anonymously. A bulletin board discusses a specific topic, and everyone who visits is welcome to share his or her viewpoint. You'll find bulletin boards on everything from Britney Spears to breast cancer to backpacking. Like chats, the main purpose of e-commerce bulletin boards is to drive traffic to a site. People who post on a bulletin board are likely to visit the site repeatedly to see other messages posted in response.

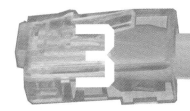

Careers Creating Content

T he people who create content for e-commerce sites have some of the most interesting jobs on the Web. If you like to read and write, to draw, or to shoot photos, content creation may be the job for you.

WRITERS AND EDITORS

According to Steve, writing e-commerce copy for the Web is the best job he has ever had. Steve works as a freelance writer, meaning that he doesn't work for one company but instead chooses assignments from many companies. Steve has an office in his apartment that he uses to write. He plans his own hours and works whenever he wants—as long as he completes his projects by their deadlines. If he wants to write all night and sleep all day, he can, and he loves that freedom. For Steve, one of the hardest things about being a freelance writer is being disciplined. It's sometimes difficult for him to make himself work when he'd rather be doing other things. But Steve knows that he has to finish his projects if he wants to get paid.

Since Steve can choose which writing projects to take, he's always working on something interesting or different. He writes marketing copy for e-commerce sites that sell all sorts of products. His life is sometimes unpredictable, but he's enjoying the freedom of being his own boss.

Web writers and editors create the text that you see on every e-commerce site that you visit. Often, a writer will create a piece for the Web that will then be analyzed and revised by an editor before it gets put on the site. Writers and editors sometimes have many of the same responsibilities. Most Web editors write copy, too, and Web writers usually do some editing.

Web writers and editors first need to have a basic understanding of the rules of language and grammar, just as they would if they were writing for a magazine or newspaper. Second, they must be able to write descriptively and enthusiastically, so that a viewer understands the product and, more important, wants to buy it. Third, they need to be able to write copy that will keep readers interested. Last, they need to have a clear understanding of the products that are being sold.

However, there's one fundamental difference between writing for print versus for the Internet. A Web writer or editor is not creating a thing—like a mail order catalog—he or she's creating an experience. The very act of reading online content is an experience for a visitor. Every piece of content on a Web site needs to lead the visitor toward the same experience—purchasing the product or service.

Web writers and editors need to understand how people behave online. They know that visitors don't like to read long pieces of information, so it's more effective to lay out text in smaller sections. They

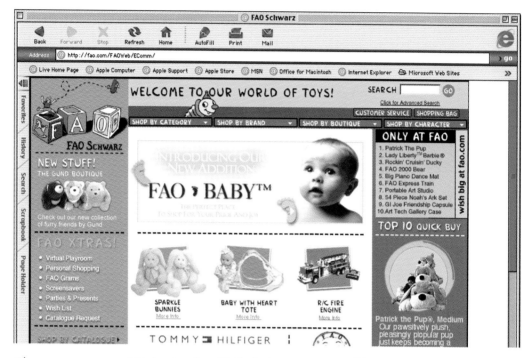

The e-commerce Web site for FAO Schwarz, a well-known toy store, uses illustrations to give its online store a "playful" presence.

also know that people jump from page to page when they surf. A writer or editor can't assume that a visitor has read something on a previous Web page. That person may not have paid attention to an earlier page or may have gotten to a page from a completely different "link," or route.

Writers and editors may create and edit original content. They may also rework content from printed material, such as mail order catalogs, to make it Web-friendly. They ensure that all the content matches the site's "voice," or tone.

ILLUSTRATORS AND PHOTOGRAPHERS

Illustration and photography are minor areas within content creation, but they're important ones. Often, illustrators and photographers also work as graphic designers.

Illustrators create drawings to be posted on a Web site. A few may draw on paper and then scan their drawings into a computer, but most illustrators work online. They use computer programs like Freehand and Illustrator to create drawings. Some may also use specialized engineering software programs to draw technical specifications, such as diagrams of automobiles, or other very complex mechanical devices that are sold on business-to-business e-commerce Web sites.

Photographers often practice both regular and digital photography. If they're doing work for an e-commerce company, though, the company will most likely want digital images. Digital photographers not only have to know the basic principles of good photography, but they also need to understand exactly how digital cameras operate. Digital photographers also need to understand complex image manipulation, or "software changing programs," which can make a product look irresistible. Using software tools like

Adobe PhotoShop, they can change an image's size, shape, color, texture, and other elements.

WEB DESIGNER

Rohini is having a much calmer day than usual—at least for now. As a Web designer for an e-commerce Web site, she's constantly updating and changing the site, often at the last minute. Because the site changes frequently, Rohini has to be able to pick up a project on a moment's notice. She spends much of her time working with Web editing and design programs like DreamWeaver and laying out pages for the site. She also works with images, using programs like PhotoShop and Illustrator. Sometimes, Rohini creates images herself, and other times she uses digital photographs or photos that she scans into her computer.

Rohini works very closely with many other departments in her company. She gets content from writers and editors, plans promotions and events with the marketing team, and relies on the computer programmers to make sure the site is running smoothly. Before a

*new portion of the site goes live, Rohini
needs to check and recheck every element.
It's crucial that the Web site is perfect, and—
with thousands of people looking at it every
day—mistakes are always noticed.*

Web designers are the people who give a Web site
its look and feel. They work very closely with Web
developers—whom you'll read about in the next
chapter—to make sure that all the separate content
elements work together well. While a Web developer
tends to have more technical responsibilities, the Web
designer usually has more creative responsibilities.

In order to create a site's "look," Web designers
need a thorough understanding of typography (the
art of using type), layout (how the page is composed),
and color. They also need to understand the differ-
ences between browsers. Browsers are the programs
that enable computers to display Web pages. A Web
page often looks different to people who use different
browsers. One of a Web designer's most important
responsibilities is to make sure that products look
good no matter the browser type.

To make a site easy for visitors to understand,
Web designers have to put text in a place where it's
easy to read and where people can find it. To make

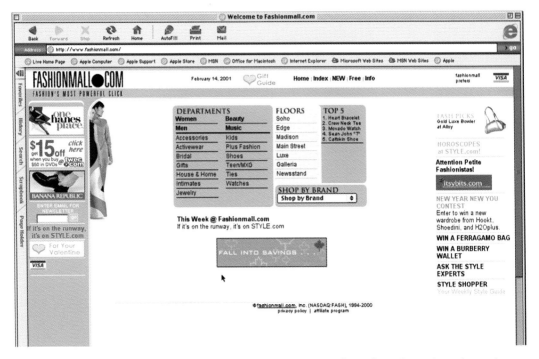

Fashionmall.com gained control of Boo.com after the short-lived Web site burned through $135 million in startup capital.

the Web site attractive, they must make sure that the images are in the right location, that they look good, and that they complement the rest of the site. Images are especially important on e-commerce sites, since visitors rely heavily on them when making purchasing decisions. Web designers use many different software programs to work with text, images, and Web pages. These can include Adobe PhotoShop, Adobe Illustrator, ImageReady, QuarkXpress, DreamWeaver, and GoLive.

E-COMMERCE CASE STUDY: BOO

Throughout the Internet world, Boo is generally thought to be an example of how NOT to run an e-commerce site. The company was founded by former fashion models Ernst Malmsten and Kajsa Leander, and funded by some of the hottest companies in fashion, including Benetton. By 1999, the upscale fashion e-tailer had raised $135 million in funding. However, because of poor management, the site wasn't able to launch when planned.

When it did launch—five months later—it was plagued by technical problems. Boo spent recklessly and burned through its funding quickly. It was forced to close only six months after its launch with $25 million in unpaid debt. Critics pointed to its poor navigation, unhelpful product descriptions, and confusing design as reasons for its failure. Fashionmall.com has recently taken over Boo and plans for a relaunch, but it hopes to manage costs more wisely. E-commerce sites, especially clothing e-tailers, have learned some important strategies from Boo's speedy demise.

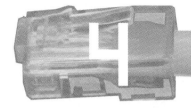

Careers Working with Content

The quality of content is important, but a successful e-commerce site also has to use content effectively. Content creation is just the beginning of the content process. Once content is created, it's up to strategists, producers, and managers to decide which content should appear on a site and how that content will be used to maximize sales.

CONTENT STRATEGISTS

Joanna loves her job as a content strategist because of the variety. Each project is different, and she's always working on new Web sites. Joanna works for a consulting company, an organization that sends employees to other companies that need help solving and completing their projects. Joanna specializes in e-commerce sites and plans all their content. In her two years as a content strategist, Joanna has built content for Web sites in the travel, entertainment, and sports e-tailing industries.

When she begins a project, Joanna spends much of her time with the client. She tries to understand exactly how the company wants the Web site to appear and to work. She attends meetings with people from all parts of the company and asks questions about its image, strategy, competitors, products, and goals for the future. It's very important that the site reflect the client as much as possible.

Next, Joanna starts mapping out a plan for the content. She decides what kind of content to use and from where to obtain it. She also creates a schedule, which explains when specific parts of the plan need to be completed, and a budget, which outlines how much the content should cost. When the plan is finished, and the client has approved it, Joanna hands it over to producers to carry out. Her work on that project is complete!

When it's time to build a Web site, content strategists are usually the first people involved in the

Creating a commercial Web site involves a schedule of planning or development, and an implementation phase.

process. Most companies—whether they're building a Web site, product, or service—divide the process into two phases. In the first phase, called the planning or development phase, the company plans the Web site, product, or service down to the smallest detail. In the second phase, called the implementation phase, the company carries out that plan. The implementation phase ends when the site "goes live," or is posted on the Internet. If the company has built a product, such as a piece of software, or a service, such as an online travel agent, the product is finally "launched," meaning it is made available to the public.

Content strategists usually work on Web sites that are being designed for the first time or that are being changed in some way. They begin a project by gaining a clear understanding of the site's purpose. To build the content, they first need to know exactly what the goal of the site is and how the company plans to accomplish that goal. For an e-commerce site, the goal is to increase sales. Strategists also need to understand who the site's customers will be and how to best communicate with them. Lastly, content strategists have to research a site's competitors—other companies that sell the same item or service and might take business away from the site. These competitors are usually other e-commerce Web sites, but they can also include brick-and-mortar companies. The strategists have to use content to make their site stand out and look better than the competition if they want to win customers away from other sites.

Once the strategists decide on the kind of content they want and how they'll use it, they research content sources and make agreements with companies to provide it. If they want original content, they find writers, photographers, and designers who can create it. Even after a Web site goes live, its content will be constantly changing. Web sites need fresh content to keep visitors returning and to feature new products, so content strategists also compare content management systems. For example, some content management systems, such as TeamSite, are computer programs that sites use to change and update their content based on their individual needs.

PRODUCERS

When the planning phase of a Web site is completed, content strategists hand over the responsibility for the plan to producers. Producers then make sure that the plan is carried out. Depending on the Web site's needs, a company will use different types of producers. The two types that work most often with content are content producers and rich media producers. Rich media refers to audio, video, and a combination of the two, which is called multimedia. Content producers usually work with all types of content, while rich media producers focus only on audio, video, and multimedia. Content producers manage the people creating the content and oversee the agreements made with content providers. Rich media producers have similar responsibilities.

Producers make sure that everyone on the project is completing his or her part of the plan as scheduled. They also need to track the costs of carrying out the plan. Every plan has a budget, or a document that outlines how much money can be spent on each part. The producers need to make sure that they're following the budget and not overspending. Producers shepherd the content and the Web site from the end of the implementation phase right through to the launch. Sometimes, they continue working on the site after the launch. Other times, they are assigned to another project and begin the process all over again.

WEB DEVELOPERS

Web developers are the people who actually "build" a Web site. They put together hundreds—and even thousands—of different items to build a single site. They are responsible for making all this separate information come together as a whole to create a successful site.

Web developers have strong technical skills but are also very creative. They need to be able to use many different types of computer languages. The Internet uses languages to communicate, just as people do. These languages tell computers what to do—to make text bigger or smaller, to put a photo

Cofounders work on developing 800hosting, which provides Web hosting, e-commerce, and Web design.

in a certain spot, or to find a piece of information and bring it back to the Web site. The most important language a Web developer needs to know is called HTML. HTML stands for hypertext markup language. It tells a Web browser what the page should look like. A Web developer uses HTML to arrange all the words, images, colors, and other items you see when you visit a site.

If you've surfed the Web lately, however, you've probably noticed that the best e-commerce sites are the interactive ones. Interactive sites move and change, and let you—the viewer—respond and interact with them. Web sites that allow you to try clothes on a virtual model, such as Lands' End, employ interactive features. Web developers use JavaScript, another useful language, to create interactive sites. HTML and JavaScript are just two of many languages Web developers use to make a Web site work properly. Other languages that they often use include C++, CGI, Java, and Perl.

COMMUNITY MANAGERS

Phuong manages the community on an e-commerce site that sells sporting goods. To attract visitors to the site—and to keep them coming back—the site also hosts chats with famous athletes and features bulletin boards about different sports. Phuong plans the chats, decides which celebrities to invite, and works with the marketing department to make sure as many people attend them as possible.

Phuong also manages the Web site's bulletin boards. When he adds a bulletin board on a new topic, he posts the first message to get the discussion started. Although Phuong has never met any of the site's visitors, he feels as though he knows them better than anyone else at the company.

43

Community is one of the best ways to draw visitors to a site. Community managers make sure that the community is doing its job successfully. They decide what type of community—bulletin boards or chats—best suits a Web site's needs. They may help to develop the community and add it to a site. Or, if the site already has a community, they work to keep it fresh and interesting.

If a Web site uses bulletin boards or chats, community managers decide what the bulletin board topics will be. They can invite an expert or celebrity to hold a chat, and participants can talk to the special guest. Or they may prefer to have "open chats," in which visitors talk to one another. A chat's success is usually measured by the number of visitors who attend, so it's very important that the chat be scheduled at a time when it can attract as many people as possible. Community managers determine chat topics and analyze data to find out when interested people are most likely to be online. They may work with the advertising department to promote the chats or bulletin boards. Because they interact directly with a site's visitors, community managers often understand its customers better than anyone else.

E-COMMERCE CASE STUDY: TARGET.COM

When it came to e-commerce, Target had a carefully thought-out plan. The brick-and-mortar discount chain wanted to start small. In 1998, Target launched a small Web site that sold only a fraction of what its stores did—about 2,000 items. Over the next two years, Target developed its e-commerce Web site and readied its warehouses and shipping facilities. The company also created extensive product descriptions and attractive product shots, and built an easy-to-use navigation system to entice visitors. In October 2000, it relaunched Target.com and increased its merchandise offering to over 15,000 items. Target.com has stiff competition, most notably Kmart's BlueLight.com and Walmart.com, but the Internet industry predicts that the site will be a success. Although many brick-and-mortar retailers raced to establish their e-commerce sites, being first doesn't always mean being best. Target's slow and steady approach may just give it the edge it needs to succeed.

Is an E-Commerce Content Career for You?

n ow that you have a better understanding of careers in e-commerce content, it's time to think about whether or not it's the life for you.

NET CULTURE

People who work for Internet companies will often tell you that the Internet isn't a job, it's a way of life. And, in many ways, they're right. The Internet industry is unlike any other. So how are Internet employees different than other people, you ask? Well, for one, they're often fairly young. The industry standard for Internet workers is only about thirty-four years old.

The Internet industry has its own personality— one that has made it famous. Companies often promote themselves as casual, fun, and filled with perks. Though this life may sound great—and it can be—it's not the complete picture. Internet workers tend to work long hours. The average Internet worker spends slightly over ten hours a day at work. And 58 percent work at least one weekend per month. Employees often trade stories about all-nighters that they've pulled at the office. The Internet culture is fast-paced, intense, and demanding, but it's also exciting, energizing, and fun.

WHAT IT TAKES TO BE SUCCESSFUL

You don't need to be a computer whiz to work for an e-commerce company. Some jobs, like software developers, programmers, and security specialists, are very technical, but others, like marketing, accounting, and administration, are not. To work with content, it's important that you like and want to learn technology, but you don't need a background in computer science to get started.

People who create and manage e-commerce content need to work well with computers and with people. No matter what your job, you'll work as part of a team. You'll need to be able to share ideas and opinions and meet deadlines. Even more important, you'll

▶ Internet workers average $84,700 in salary per year.

▶ 51 percent of Internet workers are very satisfied with their jobs.

▶ 8 percent of Internet employers allow pets at work and 7 percent offer childcare.

▶ 62 percent of Internet workers get at least three weeks of vacation a year.

▶ 88 percent of Internet workers are college graduates.

need to have good organizational and problem-solving skills. In addition, you should be open to change, since change is the nature of the Internet.

EDUCATION

You have many educational options if you're planning on an Internet career. Most employees have college degrees, and some have master's and doctoral degrees. Not sure what to study? Don't worry, you have plenty of choices. If you know that you want to work with Internet content, you may want to major in English, journalism, or a similar field. Many colleges now offer classes on writing for the Web!

If you want to pursue a technical career, you should think about majoring in engineering or computer science. However, you don't have to study computers. Because the Internet is new, many people who work in the industry have gained their knowledge on the job during or after college. Sometimes, they have degrees in unrelated fields like philosophy, political science, and even law and medicine.

Four years of college isn't your only option for an Internet education. You can also attend a two-year college and get an associate's degree. Also, many companies offer training programs and classes in technology that may last from a few weeks to a semester.

The College Question

The Internet changes quickly, and workers need to keep on top of the latest trends and technologies. Because of this, people often debate whether a young person should go to college before getting an Internet job, or just begin working after high school. Some people argue that you need a college degree to help establish a successful career. They claim that work experience can't replace a formal education.

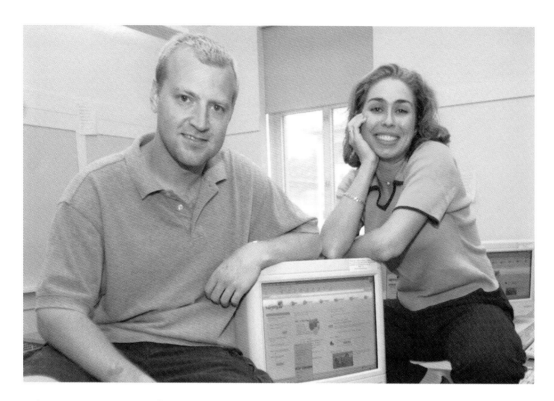

These Carnegie Mellon University students were among the first to graduate from the school with master of science degrees in electronic commerce.

Others claim that it's best to start working right away and that you can learn what you need on the job. They believe that by the time you've finished four years of college, the Internet will have changed so much that you'll already be behind.

There are no easy answers to this debate. It's true that the vast majority of Internet workers are college graduates. Employers usually prefer workers with degrees, but Internet companies are known for being flexible. In short, there's no one answer that's right for everyone.

INTERNSHIPS

Internships are a great way to find out more about an e-commerce job! If you know you want to work with the Web, you can get some valuable experience that will help you later in your career.

Most Internet companies offer internships, which can range from a few weeks to a year. Many companies even pay their interns an hourly wage, especially large ones such as Apple, IBM, and Intel, which have formal internship programs. To find out more, check the companies' Web sites. However, even small companies are usually willing to accept an intern. If you're interested in an internship but can't find one, ask someone you know at an Internet company if that organization might be interested in employing you. You'll be getting solid work experience, and you'll be giving them a very inexpensive source of labor. Everyone benefits.

THE FUTURE OF E-COMMERCE CONTENT

Five years ago, e-commerce barely existed. It's difficult to imagine what it will look like ten years from now.

Getting Started

If you're looking for some real-life Internet experience, check out the Web sites below for both internships and job opportunities.

Internships

Internship Opportunities for Students
http://www.acm.org/student/internships.html

Internship Programs.com
http://63.236.47.157/home.asp

Internweb: http://www.internweb.com

USInterns.com: http://www.USInterns.com

Jobs

CareerBuilder: http://www.careerbuilder.com

Headhunter.net: http://www.headhunter.net

HotJobs.com: http://www.hotjobs.com

Monster.com: http://www.monster.com

MediaBistro.com: http://www.mediabistro.com

Internet content is already being transformed. The wireless industry is an explosive new field that Internet companies are just beginning to explore. As wireless devices such as wireless-enabled cell phones, Palm pilots, and other PDAs (personal digital assistants) become more popular, they'll need content, too. And e-commerce companies will want to use that content to sell their products and services. Companies like AOL, OracleMobile, and Yahoo! are already creating and providing wireless content.

No one can say for sure what Internet content will look like in the future. However, everyone agrees that the demand for content is growing, as is the demand for content providers. As a young person just starting down the path toward an Internet career, you're in the perfect position!

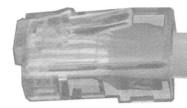

Glossary

applets Very small computer programs, such as calculators, that reside on a Web page.

browsers Programs that enable computers to display Web pages.

budget Document that outlines how much money can be spent on each part of a plan.

bulletin boards Places within a Web site where one can post messages.

business-to-business (B2B) sales Sales in which a company sells a product or service to another company.

business-to-consumer (B2C) sales Sales in which a company sells a product or service to an individual for his or her own use.

chat rooms Locations on the Internet where one can talk in real-time with live people.

click through Measure of the number of visitors who click on a product to get more information.

competitors Companies that sell the same item or service.

computer-generated images Images that have been either entirely created or significantly altered using a computer.

content All the individual pieces that are combined to make a Web site.

content management systems Computer programs that sites use to change and update their content.

digital photographs Photographs that have been converted to a digital format, which allows a computer to display them.

digital sampling Process in which a computer converts an analog sound wave to a digital sound wave.

e-commerce The practice of selling goods and services over the Internet.

HTML Hypertext markup language; it tells a Web browser what a Web page should look like.

implementation Phase in which a company carries out the plan it developed in the planning phase.

manipulation   The act of changing something.

planning   Phase in which a company plans a site, product, or service down to the smallest detail; also called the development phase.

rich media   Audio, video, or a combination of the two.

stickiness   Measure of the amount of time a visitor spends on a Web site and of how often he or she returns.

syndicate   To sell the same content to numerous buyers at the same time.

text   The written word.

typography   The art of using type.

unique visitor   A measure of the number of individual visits a Web site receives.

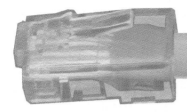

For More Information

ORGANIZATIONS

In the United States

Association of Internet Professionals (AIP)
350 Fifth Avenue, Suite 3018
New York, NY 10118
(877) AIP-0800
e-mail: info@association.org
Web site: http://www.association.org

Internet Alliance
1111 19th Street NW, Suite 1180
Washington, DC 20036-3637
(202) 956-0091
e-mail: ia@internetalliance.org
Web site: http://www.internetalliance.org

Web Design and Developers Association
(WDDA)
8515 Brower
Houston, TX 77017
(435) 518-9784
e-mail: wdda@wdda.org
Web site: http://www.wdda.org

In Canada

Canadian Association of
Internet Professionals
1335 Windrush Drive, Suite 100
Oakville, ON L6M 1W4
e-mail: info@caipnet.ca
Web site: http://www.caipnet.ca

WEB SITES

Association for Interactive Media
http://www.interactivehq.org

Association for Women in Computing
http://www.awcncc.org

Computer Professionals for
     Social Responsibility
http://www.cpsr.org

Internet Content Coalition (ICC)
http://www.netcontent.org

Internet Society
http://www.isoc.org

The Teenage Computer Network (TCN)
http://www.tcn.dhs.org/cgi-bin/tcn.pl

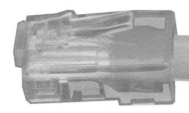

For Further Reading

Gabler, Lori. *Career Exploring on the Internet.*
  Chicago: Ferguson Publishing, 2000.
Lindsay, Dave, and Bruce Lindsay. *Dave's Quick
  'n' Easy Web Pages.* Calgary, Alberta: Erin
  Publications, 1999.
Lund, Bill. *Getting Ready for a Career as an Internet
  Designer.* Minnetonka, MN: Capstone Press, 1998.
McCormick, Anita Louise. *The Internet: Surfing the
  Issues.* Springfield, NJ: Enslow Publishers, 1998.
Perry, Robert L. *Build Your Own Website.* Danbury,
  CT: Franklin Watts, 2000.

CHALLENGING READING

Kilian, Crawford. *Writing for the Web.* Bellingham,
  WA: Self Counsel Press, 2000.
Millon, Marc. *Creative Content for the Web.* Exeter,
  UK: Intellect, 1999.

Parker, Roger C. *Roger C. Parker's Guide to Web Content and Design*. Foster City, CA: IDG Books Worldwide, 1997.

Sammons, Martha C. *The Internet Writer's Handbook*. Needham Heights, MA: Allyn & Bacon, 1999.

Tomsen, Mai-lan. *Killer Content: Strategies for Web Content and E-Commerce*. Reading, MA: Addison-Wesley, 2000.

MAGAZINES

Editor & Publisher
http://www.mediainfo.com

Grok
http://www.grok.com

Industry Standard
http://www.thestandard.com

Inter@ctive Week
http://www.zdnet.com/intweek

InternetWeek
http://www.internetwk.com

Red Herring
http://www.herring.com

Index

A

advertisers/advertising, 11, 44
Amazon.com, 6, 7
animation, 14
applets, 13
audio, 5, 10, 13, 14, 21–23, 40

B

Boo, 35
brick-and-mortar companies,
    8, 16, 39, 45
budgets, 41
bulletin boards, 13, 14, 25, 26, 44
business-to-business, 7, 31
business-to-consumer, 7

C

CDNOW, 22
chats/chat rooms, 13, 14,
    25–26, 44
click through, 11
community, 5, 13, 25, 44

community managers, 14,
    43–44
computer-generated images,
    20–21, 31–32
computer languages, 41–43
content
    what it is, 5, 6, 12, 13
    why it is important, 9–12
content creators/creation, 13,
    14, 27–35, 36
content management
    systems, 40
content producers, 14, 36,
    40–41
content providers/sources, 13,
    14, 39, 40
content strategists, 14, 36–40
content syndicators, 14
contextual commerce, 11

D

digital camera, 19

digital sampling, 21
download speed, 23

E
e-commerce
    explosive growth of, 4–5,
        7–8
    what it is, 6
education/degrees, 48–50

G
games and calculators, 13
graphic artists/designers, 20,
    31, 32–34, 39

I
illustrations, 12, 13, 20, 21, 27, 31
images, 12, 19, 31–32, 34
implementation phase, 38, 41
informational copy, 18
instructional copy, 18
interactive sites, 42–43
internships/training/jobs, 49,
    51–53

J
JavaScript, 43

L
launching a site, 38–39, 41, 45

M
marketing copy, 17–18
multimedia, 40

P
photographer/photographs,
    12, 13, 14, 19, 21, 27, 31,
    39, 41, 45
planning/development phase,
    38, 41

R
rich media producers, 14,
    40–41

S
saksfifthavenue.com, 15
selling products and services,
    4, 5, 6, 7, 9–11, 15–16,
    17–18, 23, 25–26, 29, 34
"stickiness," 11

T
Target.com, 45
teens and the Web, statistics
    on, 5, 10
text, 5, 6, 12, 13, 17–18, 28–30,
    33, 34, 41

U
unique visitors, 11

V
video, 5, 10, 13, 14, 23–24, 40

W
Web developers, 14, 33, 41–44
working conditions/salaries,
    46–48

ABOUT THE AUTHOR

As the senior content editor for HotJobs.com, Erin M. Hovanec develops content features and tools and assists with content strategy. Formerly, at ScreamingMedia, she developed content-based products and managed editorial services for *Fortune* 100 clients. She has a master's in publishing studies from New York University and a bachelor's in English from Cornell University. She is also the author of several nonfiction books for children and teens. She lives in New York City.

PHOTO CREDITS

P. 8 © buy.com; p. 12 © Kristen Artz; p. 15 © Saks Fifth Avenue; p. 20 © Barnes and Noble; pp. 24, 42, 50 © AP Worldwide Photo; p. 30 © FAO Schwarz; p. 34 © Fashionmall.com; p. 38 by Antonio Mari.

SERIES DESIGN AND LAYOUT

Les Kanturek